For K

Christmas 2020

Love,
Benny

I want you to
know and
understand us
"Mainers" better!

**STATE
OF MAINE**

STATE
OF MIND

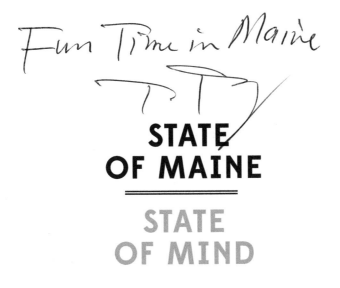

*Fun Time in Maine*

# STATE OF MAINE

### STATE OF MIND

## UPCOUNTRY HUMOR AND STORIES

### THEODORE A. PERRY

NARRATED BY T. AMONY PERKY

ILLUSTRATED BY TONE FLAVIN

STATE OF MAINE STATE OF MIND PUBLISHING

State of Maine State of Mind Publishing, Brunswick, Maine
www.stateofmainestateofmind.com
stateofmainestateofmind@gmail.com
Printed in the U.S.A.

ISBN # 9780578507637

Book design by Tom Morgan [ www.bluedes.com ]

*To all those Upcountry "Characters"*
*who fill my life with Fun and Wisdom,*
*And to Professor Walter Solmitz, of Blessed Memory*

# CONTENTS

# Preface

This book attempts to document and share with the outside world an unpretentious and wise way of life just north of the New Hampshire border, in perennial upcountry called Maine. It aims to recover local stories and discussions popular in towns like North Harmony many summers and winters ago, and still vigorous right down to the present day.

The main question, of course, is why anyone would want to live in Maine in the first place? If you were born up here, then you already know; and if you weren't, it seems that lots of you "folks from away" might be wonderin', "Why not?" For, you see, the jump from geography to real-life questions is just up the road, evoking laughter and deeper thoughts as well.

This collection of local anecdotes offers some humorous samples, and especially their underlying Maine wisdom perspectives. The hero of many of these stories, Huck Colby, was a true representative of upcountry humor and local homespun sagacity, or whatever you want to call it. Have a good laugh, and perhaps learn to think a bit more deeply while you're at it.

And if you're at all serious about simplifyin' your life, then burn your credit cards, save your cash and buy a one-way ticket.

# Introduction

Whenever I used to drive up with the kids from Connecticut to my hometown in Maine, the snickerin' started as we approached the tollbooth in Kittery, and it became almost a burst of laughter as I rolled down the window to pay the toll.

Collector at the toll: Mornin'!

Me: Ayuh, it's a real cokkah. Lots of traffic these days?

Collector: An awful lot this weekend, with the Common Ground Fair and all.

The eternal Maine question on everybody's mind, especially upon crossing the border from New Hampshire headed north, is a complex one with the simplest of answers. The question:

"You from around here?"

The answer is 100 percent objective, itself based on the deeper question:

"Where were you born?"

So, even if your family arrived to Maine on the Mayflower and has owned Indian property in Kennebunk down to this very day, or if your pregnant mother took a night out in Portsmouth, New Hampshire, and you were born prematurely in that place, then you are "from away" and not a certified Mainer. It is really all that clear and simple.

Now, suppose you *were* born here and spent much of your life "away," then what? That is the case with me, T. Amony Perky, and that is why the kids always had such fun as we approached the tollbooth in Kittery. Nothin' truer than that old saw in all our hearts, "You can take me out of Maine, but you can't take Maine out of me."

I want to allow right here that this "Maine" condition of mine might have disadvantages, of course, but this single thing puts me ahead of all the fakes out there. Some out-of-staters are quite clever at this game, the most successful being, I suppose, those two fellas who put Maine on the storytelling map, so to speak: Bert and I. They even fooled *me* when I heard them speak at Yale many years ago. Mainers to the bone, you might surmise. Well, okay, then. But definitely *not* Mainers like me, T. Amony Perky. In my case there are extra advantages as well; not only that I speak *both* languages, Mainese and Connecticutese, but, in fact, even a third, if you rightfully include that beautiful Canuck

(French-Canadian) version. And even with all that, I am not all the way "home," either, since I never did learn any of our Native American languages. But that's another story, a tragic one by my way of thinkin'. *C'est très tragique, non?* I'll try to expand things a bit in some of the anecdotes that will follow.

*       *       *

And now meet Dad's Old Friend from upcountry Maine.

A few summers back, Dad took me to see his old childhood friend, Huck Colby. Rumor had it that Huck had cancer and was on his way out. I hadn't seen him in years, but fondly remembered those fishing trips up Jackman way, back when the streams were full of trout and folks had nothing better to do than go fishin'. I also remembered that Huck loved to talk about the old days, about people, about how he saw life. "Just open your eyes wide and there it is," he used to quip.

Well, Huck was in one of his talkative moods that day, and on the following days as well. We had such a good time that we just kept coming back for more. I recorded some of his stories, but mostly I just try to recall things he said, and his tone of voice—oh, Lordy, that Maine twang and love for one-liners that made you smile and sit up and think about things in a slightly different way! Of course, Huck never thought of himself as wise, just having lots of fun. And this leads us to the theme of this collection.

## EDWARD BALDWIN SELF (1910-2002), HUSBAND
## BEATRICE BELLENGER SELF (1918-2008), WIFE
## DON'T WE HAVE FUN!

This tombstone inscription records the final message of an Indian couple assessing their achievements and goals of living. The first "funny" point about this epitaph is the circumstances: Mr. and Mrs. Self say that they are having fun as they lie here deceased! The use of the present tense alters the perspective, however, focusing on the broader and even universal "we," what all of us are to be doing at all times. The human condition is to have fun, and Fun, Life, is with people. Also, notice the punctuation—not the doubt of a question, but rather the congratulatory and assertive backslapping of one another: "My, don't we [all] have fun!" The geographical location that both preserves and projects this ideal is crucial as well: the Indian Burial Ground of the Wampanoag Tribe in Chappaquiddick, Massachusetts. Like Massachusetts, Maine, as well (we formed one single state until 1820), shares a diversity of ethnic origins.

This Native American couple has been chosen as our guest of honor: for their Native American ancestry, their open and expansive Maine/New England territorial perspectives, and their inclusive gift of having fun. Looking back over things and recalling any one of the peculiarities and difficulties of everyday life, Huck loved to quote his grandmother, "We had nothing, but we had fun!" So, too, with Huck's sense of humor: a matter-of-factness based on the everyday and everyone we are invited to share it with, without any sense of entitlement or anger that arises there-from. In sum, "Just livin' is far from perfect, but do get back to me if you find anything better."

Huck's upcountry focus also expands the usual background a bit. A half-century ago, Maine wisdom humor was typically a coastal and Down East event, with all the *lobstahs* you could eat. Huck came from another Maine, the upcountry one with forested mountains and valleys, freshwater and loons and moose, maple sugar and plantings: a living space with four full seasons that allow worthwhile reapings, each in its own time.

Anyhow, here are some Huck stories pretty much the way he said 'em, plus a lot more that Dad and I gathered. Hope you like 'em too! We are going to have some fun, no?

—*T. Amony Perky (TAP)*

P.S. Huck asked me to change the names, "to protect the guilty."

# Welcome to Maine

# THE WAY LIFE SHOULD BE?

When you drive into Maine up Interstate 95, right over the border there is a sign that reads:

"Welcome to Maine, the Way Life *Should* Be."

Huck Colby, the local sage and hero of many of these anecdotes, recalled how there were originally not one but three versions of that road sign. Here is the first:

"Welcome to Maine, the Way Life *Could* Be."

He thought that this was pointed at out-of-staters but didn't really work for natives. So they came up with another version:

"Welcome to Maine, the Way Life *Is*."

Then they compromised and came to the one they have now:

"Welcome to Maine, the Way Life Should Be."

Huck thought that it all didn't matter that much, because the last two mean the same thing:

The way life *is* up here is the way life should be.

# GOODNUFF FOR A LIFETIME

To further encourage visitors to Maine, the advertising people came up with another tag:

"Maine: Good for a Visit. Good for a Lifetime."

Huck had a slightly different take on all that as well, a kind of a "not yet" reaction. He opined that the one doesn't necessarily lead to the other, unless you already know how it is all going to work out in the end. Sure enough, if the visit was good, then the full picture can't be *all* bad. Folks up here know that. For even if the bad outweighs the good—maybe a friend is in the hospital or the fish aren't biting today—Mainers (including those out-of-staters who decide to stay on) usually end up most days feeling that it is surely "goodnuff." So maybe tweak it just a bit the next time around:

"Maine: Good for a Visit. Good *Enough* for a Lifetime."

# FAIR WEATHER ON COMMON GROUND

Every year since creation—or at least since Prohibition—everyone looked forward to the Windsor County Fair. It was easy to remember because it always fell on Labor Day. Or maybe it was the other way around. That's what Huck thought anyway:

"Labor Day always occurs during the Windsor Fair."

Two things were especially fun at the fair. I recall that most of the games were run by out-of-staters who just didn't know Maine folks all that well. Father used to be a pitcher for the North Harmony Grange team. He could throw a stone and hit a white birch trunk from fifty feet as often as he wanted. Well, you remember those fairground games where you win stuffed animals for knocking down wooden bottles with a baseball? Father always ended up with enough birthday presents for all the kids in the family, and then some. It was when they would pay Father *not* to play that we all sensed our native superiority.

The other fun things were the big white helium balloons. Huck never got his own because they cost twenty-five cents, but he always enjoyed hearing them pop with such a loud noise. And, strangely enough, the balloons always waited to burst until Huck was right up close. Probably so that he could hear them pop better.

There is a new fair up Maine way. Used to be on the Windsor Fair grounds, but they have moved down the road to Unity. It has no horse racing, no Ferris wheel, nothing much at all, except food and agricultural produce. It is called the Common Ground Fair. Huck calls it an "old-fashioned" fair because, he explains, "that's the way fairs used to be: nothing to do except eat and chew the fat of the land."

Huck recommends it, "It could change your life."

# Growin' Up in Maine and Growin' Up the Kids

## SPOILIN' THE KIDS

Most folks up in Maine spoil their kids something awful. Huck said he knew why:

"Even if they die young, they will still have most of the joys and few of the pains. Then, too, if they have no pains, they won't grow up . . . So, I guess they will just have to grow up!"

Years later, Huck put it this way:

"Some cranks think they have to punish kids, but I guess they never heard the old proverb, the one that says, 'Spare the child and spoil the rod!'"

# DON'T EAT THE CANDY

Huck's grandmother spoiled him something wicked. When he had just barely learned to walk, he would run up and down the sidewalk, spitting at anyone who came by. Auntie T. would get mad as hell, but Grammie would yell back:

"Don't you dare hit that child!"

When Huck got his first teeth, the spitting became bites, but it was still:

"Don't you dare hit that child!"

Huck always liked to tell this story. He claimed that this is where he learned self-confidence. He also argued that it taught the neighbors respect.

"One day I bit old Isaiah Manson so hard the blood came. The very next day he brought me a piece of candy."

P.S. Huck's grandmother instructed him to thank old Isaiah, but she refused to let him eat the candy.

## NICE ICE CREAM CONES

I asked Huck about his fondest childhood memory and he chose this one:

"When I was about five—it was a hot summer evening—Mother did the supper dishes a bit early, dried her hands on her apron, finished the ironing, and said, 'Huck, let's walk down to the corner and get a nice ice cream cone.'

Mother took my hand and we walked down to the corner. I had vanilla and she had strawberry. On the way back, she told me all about the old days when she was growing up."

Don't we have fun up here!

# Copin' and Makin' Do

# HUCK'S WOODEN LEG

There are lots of stories about how Huck lost his leg, but this is the true one, as far as I can tell.

Before refrigerators were invented, did you ever wonder how they used to keep the milk nice and cool during the summer heat? They got the ice from Soapy Joseph! But have you ever wondered where Soapy Joseph got the ice? Soapy got the ice during the winter, when Webber Lake was frozen deep. They'd cut the ice with big saws and Soapy would put it all in his barn under tons of sawdust.

Huck was the one who used to man the saw that cut the ice. He slipped just once and lost his left leg up to the knee. He picked himself up and was so damned mad he threw the leg right at the saw.

"That's a funny thing to do with a leg," Billy Johnson observed.

Sometimes Huck would joke about it and say, "I just never saw the saw."

# HOUDINI HUCK

Well, Huck got himself a wooden leg and knew he'd never play high school football again. But the very next winter he was back out cutting ice. Not only that; rather than feel bad about the loss, Huck was now persuaded that his brand-new leg gave him special magical powers.

As a kid, Huck had always loved those tricks of Harry Houdini, the famous magician, remember him? Now he started thinking about how he could also perform such feats, especially for all those kids in town who just loved their Uncle Huck.

His signature trick was to convince kids—and himself to boot—that the leg itself had magical powers. For this to happen, everyone thought—or wanted to—that the replacement part was still, well, alive. Huck had not really lost the original one. From his lively behavior, one would think that he was only a bit lame but otherwise okay, and that the crutch was merely for balance. But it was far more than that; it also granted Huck special powers that other legs just did not possess. The leg was not only still real enough, it was now super-real.

So, one school day Huck was invited to his granddaughter's grammar school to perform a few of his Houdini tricks for the kids. He asked one of the kids for a well-sharpened wooden pencil. He lifted his own pant leg halfway up to the knee, and then drove the pencil right through the flesh, and even bone, until it came out the other side of the leg. He then wiggled the pencil back and forth, in and out a few times, before pulling it out, bloodless, and handing it back to the students for inspection. The kids could not believe their eyes!

What Houdini Huck had prepared, of course, was a well-drilled hole, carefully concealed by both his high socks and baggy pants.

# JOHNNY DEROSBY

Huck tells about how his good friend Johnny Derosby used to buy up old pianos and fix 'em up. One year his wife Anne had triplets—three little girls who remained awfully cute even though they all wore glasses. Johnny went right out and found four pianos:

"Just in case we would all want to play at the same time."

When the girls got older and needed more room, Johnny sold the pianos. He explained:

"Nobody ever wrote a piece for eight hands."

## 6/12

One of the great plagues of human existence, at least upcountry, is the blackflies. They start up right after ice is out in May and last until they damn please, which is usually about three weeks into June. Up Jackman way they say that it takes only a dozen black-flies to carry off a normal-size human being. The main problem is, no repellent seems to work: The flies like 'em all!

Well, Huck heard of a new concoction called 6/12, which had become very popular with the out-of-state crowd. His conclusion:

"It took me a full week to figure out how to use the stuff, then I got the trick: You just spray a full bottle on a tree stump about fifty feet away and all the blackflies in the area will rush to the stump."

# The Way It Is

# REDOING THE KITCHEN

When Beatrice Latulip had her kitchen redone, Huck's wife Esther got the idea she wanted hers redone too. Huck said he'd look into it. Every morning after breakfast Huck would pour himself an extra cup of coffee and just sit there staring the kitchen up and down. Then he would get up and walk around it in all directions. Then he would sit down again, deep in thought.

This went on for quite some time. Then one day Huck announced his new plan for the kitchen:

"As my Old Man used to say, 'It's fine just the way it is.'"

From that day on, the family just seemed to enjoy the old kitchen even more than before. Whenever the matter came up with one of the kids or younger relatives, Huck liked to point out the following:

"You can get the new stuff anytime you want, but the old stuff?"

He would clinch his argument with a question:

"When is the last time you were comfy in a rocking chair?"

Nobody seemed to understand what Huck meant by that except the old folks, and they didn't need to be told.

# FINGERS

When Huck and Esther had been married thirty-some years, they thought it would be nice to get wedding rings. After looking in all the jewelry stores in Portland, they decided not to get rings. Huck explained:

"If you've got fingers, why would you need rings? And if you don't, where would you put 'em?"

## HOLDING THE ROAD

George V. and his brother-in-law Charles were always kidding one another. George needed an old car to drive around in, and Charles said he could have his for $100. Now Charles wanted to get rid of his jalopy, because it didn't have any suspension springs in the rear. So he drove out to the quarry and filled the trunk full up with stones.

The next day George put down the $100 and drove off in his new car. On his way home he stopped off at the corner grocery store to stock up. He walked out to his car with his arms full of groceries and opened up the trunk: not a damned spot for the groceries!

George still decided to keep the car:

"Not much room for groceries, but it sure does hold the road nice."

# The "...," or Speechless Factor

The "..." factor (speechless reaction or response) is prevalent in Maine, but it seems to occur a bit more in those areas bordering away-land or in the presence of out-of-staters. This might lead to speculation as to whether Mainers are really all *that* speechless. Perhaps they are just kidding around, making fun of the from-away people. Or, perhaps both. The trick of "..." in most cases is to figure out just who is being made fun of. "..." can also occur among locals, where it is rarely explicit but often implied.

# THE WINE MENU

Last summer Joe Vigue's brother-in-law Barry and his missus came up for a short visit all the way from New Jersey. Traveling north, they stopped at a local diner just off I-95 in Maine.

Barry: Do you have a wine menu?

Waitress: Ayuh.

Barry, ten minutes later: Are we ever going to get that wine menu?

Waitress: You didn't ask for it.

Barry: . . .

# A HARD ROLL, PLEASE

This tourist walked into a deli/bakery in Livermore Falls around noontime.

Tourist: I'd like some butter and jam on a hard roll, please.

Waitress: Sorry, you will have to come back tomorrow for that.

Tourist: But I see some rolls over there, fresh out of the oven.

Waitress: Sure enough. But it takes a whole day for 'em to get hard.

Tourist: . . .

# AT THE PORTLAND
# TRAIN STATION

Huck: I'd like a ticket to Boston.

Agent: There's a special this week. One-way is only $6, round-trip is $15.

Huck: I'll have two returns, please.

Agent: . . .

# DIVINE YOU SAY?

Huck stopped by his lawyer's office in Augusta to pick up some documents. A new woman was tending the reception desk.

Huck: I haven't seen you before. You from around here?

Secretary: Yes, indeed. I'm third-generation here.

Huck: What is the family name?

Secretary: I am married to Charles Doble.

Huck: That's a strange one. But what is *your* family name?

Secretary: It's Divine.

Huck: . . . But what is your family *name?*

Secretary: Hey, that's a cokkah!

# VANILLA CAKES

During Prohibition folks were especially interested in the recreational properties of such products as vanilla, bay rum, Sterno . . . Well, one morning John Daley walked into the grocery store. He seemed to be walking slightly tippy-toed and as much sideways as forward.

Daley: I'd like a bottle of vanilla, please. Mary wants to make me a birthday cake.

He took the vanilla, carefully folded the charge slip, and headed for the door. Then he paused and turned back.

Daley: Come to think of it, better let me have another bottle: Mary may want to make me *two* birthday cakes.

Grocer: . . .

# Makin' Fun
# (of Out-of-Staters)

# DAMN THE DAM

One of the major events in recent Maine history is the removal of the dam on the Kennebec River in Augusta, transforming a sewer into a magnificent fishing river. Not only are the native fish restored, but the ocean is sending up blues and shad and stripers as far as Waterville, and even beyond. This means that lots of out-of-staters are coming up to fish—an endless source of fun for local people.

Just recently, for example, this fella from Connecticut cast way out and got his line hooked on the bottom. A local fisherman cautioned:

"You may well have hooked on to a halibut there. Some as big as two, three hundred pounds have been spotted up here. The main thing is not to pull too hard and snap the line. And remember that such a big fish can take a long time to land."

It did.

## TROUT FISHING RENEWED

Now that the trout are coming back to Maine, out-of-staters are also coming up in greater numbers. One day Huck stopped off at L.L.Bean's in Freeport on his way back from Portland:

"The place was full of folks buying the damnedest contraptions you ever saw!"

He coined a saying right then and there:

"You can buy fish at Hannaford's Market for $5 a pound, or you can go out to L.L.Bean's and then try to catch your own for $40 a pound."

# MAINE CHANCE FARM

When Huck was a young man he worked summers at Maine Chance Farm in Mount Vernon, Maine. Huck explained:

"That's the spa where rich out-of-stater women used to come up Maine way and spend lots of money not to eat."

Huck got a big kick out of those folks:

"They put as much effort into spending money as I do in earning it!"

When the Maine Chance ladies weren't dieting, they spent hours on those exercise machines. That also tickled Huck:

"These out-of-staters have so little to do and so much time to do it in! What's weird is that they think exactly the opposite."

## LEMON IN YOUR TEA?

Huck went all the way to Florida to see his distant cousin, Flora, who lived most all her life down there and made herself quite a bit of money in some kind of industry. After dinner in the garden (as they do down there), Flora asked if anyone would like lemon in their tea. Huck just reached up behind him and started to pick one from the tree.

Flora: "Hold on a minute!"

She rushed to the kitchen and brought out a plastic lemon. Huck had two squirts and then remembered he preferred coffee.

# Goin' Fishin'

# A WAY OF LIFE

Fishing means, as you would expect, going outside to some kind of water and, well, attempting to catch fish. If you were a commercial fisherman, though, that would be simply "fishing," for food or money, most likely. "*Going* fishin'" is another ball game entirely, a distinct way of life, which of course might still involve water and displacement away from the home environment.

So, for example, whenever Huck wanted to go fishing, he just, well, up and went fishin'. One of the summer folks was puzzled:

"We can't figure it, Huck. You don't even eat the fish!"

Huck: "Who says I go fishin' to catch fish?"

Everyone in North Harmony would understand that remark.

# PERSONAL PRIVACY

After the war Esther Colby took a job in some office to help pay for the new washing machine and other stuff. She worked afternoons from 1:00 to 5:00 p.m.

One day she came home at 6:30 p.m. and Huck was upset. She explained that one of the bosses from Connecticut had some extra work for her to finish. Huck was mad as hell:

Huck: If I were a lawyer, I'd sue!

Esther: On what grounds?

Huck: Invasion of privacy.

# A DECLARATION OF
# INDEPENDENCE AT PIERCE POND

These Connecticut fellas wanted to catch some good old red-belly Maine brook trout, so Huck sent them up to Pierce Pond in Somerset County. He told them to look up a registered Maine Guide named Steve Colby, who he thought was a distant relative.

Steve happened to be there the day they arrived, but he already had a party of fishermen to take out on the pond.

"Well, Mr. Colby, at least give us your phone number, and we'll call you next year when we come up," the fellas said.

"Can't do that. I may want to go fishin' myself that day," Steve answered.

## BURNED TO THE GROUND; INSTANT RECOVERY

Last July the Colbys' barn burned to the ground. The fire was over by about noontime. Esther was upset:

"Huck, you've got to get right over to the bank and ask for a loan."

Huck, picking up his fishing gear:

"I don't know about all that, but I'll be home for supper the usual time. And don't forget the beets."

# Work You Say?

## CLEARING THE TABLE

When they think you have finished your meal and want to clear your table, waitresses in upcountry restaurants often ask the customers:

"You still workin' [i.e., on that food]?"

Huck's typically surprised response:

"Work?! Never worked a day in my life."

## LAZINESS

Huck had a reputation for being lazy but never let it upset him.

"If I started worrying about that, I'd have *two* problems," he'd say.

# MILL'S DOWN

One Friday Rocky Plourde showed up at the mill around ten a.m. The boss was standing at the door:

Boss: Rocky, what the hell are you doing here today? The mill is down!

Rocky: Oh, I just came by to help out Chester Blodget.

Boss: What's *he* doing here today?!

Rocky: Nothin' much.

## GRANDPA JOE'S GARDEN

When Huck's grandfather got old, his wife Beattie used to plague him every spring:

Beattie: Joe, you goin' to plant again this year?

Joe: Ayuh.

Beattie: But why, Joe? It's so damn much work!

Joe: Yup, but I don't feel much like livin' if I don't have my garden.

The next year she commanded him *not* to plant his garden, but he did anyhow.

Beattie died that fall.

## SITTING ON THE STOOP: MAKING SPACE FOR OTHERS

Not long ago, Huck's teenage grandson came up from Connecticut to spend a week. After a few hours the kid was restless:

Grandson: Not much going on up here! What do you do with your time?

Huck: Not all that much. But we ain't bored.

Grandson: Well, what did you do when you were my age?

Huck: Sat on the back stoop and picked our noses, mostly.

Grandson: If that's true, then why do you all have such small noses?

Huck: Because we don't stick 'em much into other people's business, I suppose.

# Beware of Thy Neighbor!

# THE ICEBOX

Every Tuesday and Friday afternoon about 4 p.m., Soapy Joseph came by to deliver ice for the icebox.

Mrs. Colby: Been awfully hot these past few days. Better give me ten cents' worth.

Soapy sized up the pieces, chose one for Mrs. Colby, and carefully wiped away most of the sawdust.

Soapy: That will be ten cents, please.

Mrs. Colby: . . .

When Mrs. Colby walked back into the house with her ice, she started to wonder:

Mrs. Colby: Hmmm! Never heard old Soapy say 'please' before.

The very next day, Mrs. Colby went out to Monkey Wards and bought herself a brand-new electric 'frigerator, one that even made ice cubes. She reasoned:

"At least now I won't be throwing away all that money on someone who never said 'please' before."

# MAY SPECIAL

A few years back, in the month of May, Huck's father drove up to the hospital to get some information. So many of his friends were having their prostate removed, he figured they might be having a special that month. He found out that although he didn't have cancer, an operation would still give him a better night's sleep because he wouldn't have to get up a half-dozen times to pee. It sounded good to him, and he had it done.

Folks were curious about how it all worked out. He explained that this operation was his first, and dammit, his last, too. But, for all that, it did have its advantages:

"Instead of six times a night, I only get up four or five times now. That is quite an improvement over the course of a lifetime. And the best thing is that, if and when I do die, it won't be from prostate cancer, like Frank Vigue."

## DAY IN COURT AND
## LEARNING THE TRADE

Huck got caught poaching deer, which means shooting 'em out of season. The judge was mad as hell:

Judge: Mr. Colby, you will pay the State of Maine $35 in fines, and you will lose all your deer.

Huck: That's fine, Your Honor. But who will feed the wife and kids if you take away my money and food?

Judge: Well, I'll let you off this time, but don't you let me catch you doing that again.

Huck: Don't worry, Your Honor. You won't.

And the judge never did.

# SWIMMING LESSON

Huck learned to swim down at Lombard's Dam when someone pushed him in over his head. He wasn't mad a bit:

"I still had the choice of swimming or not."

He added:

"As the old folks used to say about most everything, you always do have a choice, you know."

# Money

## THANKSGIVING SALES

The day after Thanksgiving was supposed to have the biggest sales of the entire year. Esther decided to go shopping:

Esther: "I'll save $10 on that coat I always wanted."

Huck: "And if you don't go shopping at all, you'll save $50."

# CREDIT CARDS

When credit cards came out, Huck decided to inquire.

Banker: How much money do you have in the bank, Mr. Colby?

Huck: None.

Banker: Well, now, how much money do you *have*?

Huck took out a wad of bills out of his front pocket: Let's see . . . $764 and change.

Banker: You'd better put that money in a checking account and get a credit card!

Huck: Why?

Banker: So you can pay your bills.

Huck: I don't have any.

Huck walked out of the bank without a credit card.

"The way I figure it, I don't need one," he said to himself. And he added, with a chuckle: "Unless I want to pay all those bills that I don't have."

# FOR YOUR CONVENIENCE

Esther drove Huck crazy for years until he agreed to open a bank account. They decided on the local Savings Institution.

A few weeks later, the Institution moved out of Main Street and relocated in the mall out of town, explaining that this was "for your greater convenience."

The very next day Huck went in to close out his account. When the banker asked why, Huck explained:

"I'm doing it for my *own* greater convenience."

# BEER SALT

The old folks used to pour a glass of beer and sprinkle in some salt before drinking it. When Huck went down to Connecticut, he ordered a glass of beer and asked for the salt. Everybody at the table laughed like hell and Huck couldn't understand why.

With the meal they brought some Italian water in a green bottle. Huck took a sip and spit it out. He thought that salt tasted better in the beer than in the water.

He was also surprised that the water cost more than his beer.

# WEALTH

Huck never seemed to work much but always had enough to get by, and even to have cash on hand. He explained that there are only two ways to have money:

"You can earn it, or you can not spend it."

Then he got really pensive:

"My sister down in Connecticut thinks that you have to *spend* it in order to have it. They call it advertising."

# POVERTY

This reporter from Hartford asked Huck why there are so many poor people in Maine.

Huck: "When I was a kid growing up, everybody in town was poor, but we didn't know that until later. Because, as I said, in those days *everybody* was poor."

He then reflected:

"Hold on there. Sounds strange, doesn't it? When everybody is poor, then nobody is. When only some are poor, then there are so damned many poor people you can't even count 'em. Hmmm . . . We'd better hire some smart politician from Hartford to think about that one."

# At Home

# AT HOME, DAMMIT!

Back in the early '50s it was hard getting around town. Folks didn't use horse and buggy much anymore, and cars were awfully expensive. Edmund L. decided it was time to start up a taxi service. He bought a jalopy and fixed it up pretty good. Since there was a pay-phone booth right at the four corners, that is where Edmund used to park his cab and wait for calls.

One day the phone rang and Edmund answered:

Edmund: Ed's Taxi Service!

Woman's voice: Edmund, come pick me up.

Edmund had no idea who it was, so he waited for a call back. About forty-five minutes later, the phone rang again:

Woman's voice: Edmund, are you going to come and pick me up or not?

Edmund: Where are you?

Woman's voice: I'm here at home, dammit!

And she hung up again.

## LOCATION, LOCATION

Last week this fella from some big magazine came up to find out about Maine folks. Lucky for him, he found his way to Huck.

Reporter: Mr. Colby, where did you grow up?

Huck: On the porch.

Reporter: On *the* porch! Which one?

Huck: The one in front of my house, of course.

## TRAVELING THE MAINE CENTRAL RAILROAD

Huck had quite a reputation in town as a traveler, although he didn't like to brag about it much. He regularly went down to Togus (near Augusta), but maybe that didn't count, because it was always to see his cousin at the VA hospital. He and Esther went shopping in Portland once in a while, and he just *loved* to go down to Fenway and watch the mighty Ted Williams lob the ball out of the park. He even made it down to New York City and Florida once.

Huck: "It used to be a lot easier to go places in the old days because of the Maine Central Railroad, which had passenger service to almost anywhere you wanted to go. Not that folks used it all that much—mostly because Mainers like to stay close to home well enough. But we still loved our train, because you *could* go somewhere if you ever wanted to."

# STREETS

Huck Colby came back from Boothbay Harbor. He said that there were just too many streets:

"How can you find anyone unless you know the name of the street?"

He looked all afternoon for Charley Smith, but folks kept asking him where he lived.

"That's what I'm asking *you*," he replied.

He added that in North Harmony things were much simpler. Either you lived on Main Street or on RFD (Rural Free Delivery). If you wanted Sam Laplante on Main Street, you just went to my grandfather's barbershop at the four corners and there he was. If you wanted someone on RFD, you just headed out of town and sooner or later you found him.

## SUPPERTIME IN HEAVEN

Huck had a favorite hymn called, "When It's Suppertime in Heaven." Dad and I heard it one Saturday evening on the radio. It was sung by a few Maine hillbillies, and made us laugh like hell.

But Huck explained:

"They call heaven 'suppertime' because that's the best part of the day—the time everyone gets together at home and you talk about the day and make plans for the next. What could be more heavenly than that?"

# True Love

## . . . AND TOENAILS

One day Dad walked into Esther's kitchen to find her cutting Huck's toenails. He left and returned ten minutes later, and now it was Huck cutting Esther's. Dad claims that, before that day, he never understood Huck's description of love. He asked:

"In your life how many people are there you can ask to cut your toenails?"

Huck surmised that you could recognize out-of-staters by the fact that they cut their own toenails. Or pay to have them cut.

# PAHSNIPS IN THE SOUP

One day Esther Colby was in the kitchen making chicken soup when Huck walked in.

Huck: Esther, what did you put in that soup?

Esther: Pahsnips.

Huck: Esther, you know I don't like pahsnips.

Esther: Well, I like pahsnips. Always did. Always will.

Huck: Well, I hate pahsnips. Always did. Always will.

Esther: You can't make chicken soup without pahsnips, Huck.

Huck: Why not?

Esther: Pa used to say that chicken soup *has* to have pahsnips.

Huck: Well, Esther, you go ahead with the pahsnips in the damn soup.

Esther: Will you eat it, Huck?

Huck: I'll eat the soup . . . But I won't eat the pahsnips.

# CHEMO

Joe Fitzpatrick ran into Huck down at the hardware store. Joe had shaved off all his hair.

Huck: You got cancer?

Joe: Nope. My daughter Nancy does.

## GOOD-BYE AND HALLOOO

Huck tells about this old duffer in North Harmony who always walked down Main Street with a smile. He didn't remember his name, just the smile. He also recalled the way he said hello, before anyone else could say it:

"Hallooo!"

Before Huck's aunt Beattie died, she lay in bed for weeks crying about her pains because of the cancer, or so everyone said. But when she gave up her last breath, that old smile forced itself upon her face and from her deepest chest came a long

"Halloooo."

# TWO OR THREE

Beatrice and Harry were having an argument. Harry left the house, came down to the barbershop, and tried to figure out just why people fight. The wisdom was pretty thick that day. Someone thought Harry did right by leaving the house, since

"It takes *two* to fight."

Most everyone agreed, but some also disagreed, since

"It also takes two to make love."

The session ended in deep silence when Huck proposed:

"Yes, but it sometimes takes *three* to make peace."

# Aging

# FEELING 'BOUT THE SAME

At his eighty-second birthday party Huck spoke a few words:

"Today I am eighty-two years old. I feel eighty-two and I look eighty-two, and that's just lovely. For over thirty years Pa always had the same answer as to how he was feeling today:

'Oh, 'bout the same.'

When I called to wish him a happy birthday on his eighty-fifth and asked how he was feeling, he answered:

'Oh, not so bad.'

He died the next day."

Huck went on to talk about olden times:

"Life was awfully hard in the old days. My grandfather looked eighty-two when he was sixty. From all the work on the farm and the mill to boot, Emma Smith stopped looking sexy when she was fifty, if not before. Nowadays the world is upside down and that's maybe all for the better. I mean that at eighty-two, people want to look fifty, and I suppose it won't be long before people at one hundred will want to look twenty!"

Huck smiled and made one of those wise expressions:

"At that rate folks at a hundred and twenty will not even be born yet. Or they will be so long dead that they won't be able to tell the difference."

# MINDING YOUR LOSSES

Everybody always looked forward to the high school reunion every five or so years. It was a time when you got to hear what people were doing with their lives, and the food was awfully good, too. One of the best parts was the "roundtable discussion" that they always had after supper. At this particular reunion, Frank Giroux had just had his prostate removed and they all thought this would be a good topic.

There were six people at the table, plus, of course, the moderator. He asked the first question:

Moderator: "What would you rather lose, your prostate or your legs?"

George G., who was a lumberjack from up north, said right out:

"Your damned prostate, of course."

The moderator persisted: "Your legs or your eyes?"

Fred, who fancied himself a picture painter: "Your legs."

Moderator: "Your eyes or your mind?"

Francine Boudreau, the seventh-grade teacher: "Your eyes, of course."

Moderator: "Your mind or your soul?"

Pastor: "For God's sake, your mind!"

Huck jumped right up from his chair: "I vote for Francine, because if you lose your mind, aren't you dead already? And if you have your head, what else do you really need?"

# PUSHING SEVENTY

As he approached his seventieth birthday, Huck would say how he was always on the edge of tears lately. Dad asked him why that was, and here was Huck's reply:

"There could be three reasons. Either I've got cancer, or I'm very well, or we don't have enough damn wood to get through the winter."

Dad also asked Huck what he thought about heaven:

Huck: "My fantasy is to retire there," he replied.

Then he quickly added:

"Unless I am needed elsewhere."

## OLD GEORGE AT A STANDSTILL

Friend: "Old George ain't what he used to be!"

Huck: "Never was."

# Dyin' and Thereabouts

# A TIME TO DIE

The pastor was fond of quoting King Solomon's verse:

"There is a time to live and a time to die."

Huck, of course, put his own spin on that one:

"Dyin' won't take much time or effort, but I just never do find enough time to live."

When his wife Esther heard him say this, she went out and bought him a birthday present: a brand-new watch.

## PREPARING TO DIE

Huck sent $200 for Christmas to his poor aunt Leah in Vermont. He worried:

"She is dying of lung cancer and can't even afford snow tires for the winter."

## WHY WE DIE: THE CASE OF BABY JOCELYN

Jocelyn Proulx died at age three. At the funeral the pastor noted:

"We all must die sooner or later."

Huck was heard to mumble under his breath:

"Well, I'd prefer later myself."

From that day on he never went back to church. When asked why not, he explained:

"I don't mind dyin', but I wouldn't want to stay around for the sermon."

The very next day there was a lively discussion at the corner store. Someone said that Jocelyn died because her mother led a bad life. The grocer thought that the family didn't eat all that well. Someone else observed that the father never went to church. Huck wondered if it wasn't because Baby Jocelyn had pneumonia.

## LIVIN' ON A BIT LONGER: AUNT MARY'S FUNERAL

When Aunt Mary died, Huck drove all the way down to Rhode Island for the funeral.

"Hadn't seen her for twenty years, and I wanted to have a last visit."

On the way back he stopped at a diner for apple pie and coffee. When he got back home, he was pleased with the trip:

"They got TV down there. The funeral was beautiful. And the apple pie was so damn good, they must have got the recipe from my Aunt Mary."

# DYIN' AND THEREAFTER:
# HAROLD ALFOND

You have all heard of Dexter shoes, right? Harold Alfond, their founder and owner, was treated for his lung cancer at the very hospital in Augusta that he had built and financed. One day Huck went by the cancer center to see his neighbor, Doris Beaulieu, and there was Harold right in the next bed! Harold, of course, had money enough to get treated anywhere, but he chose his own home environment.

Huck got the point:

"Harold decided that if it was good enough for his lifelong Maine neighbors, then it was good enough for him as well. As he was fond of saying, he wanted to 'give back to the people of Maine' for giving him such a wonderful life. So, he decided to stick around a bit longer, by setting up a trust that gives to all children born in Maine the beginnings of a fund to finance their college education."

Huck reflected: "With that kind of money flying around up here, I hope that Massachusetts has some regret about splitting from Maine back in 1820 . . ."

# MRS. JONES'S PASSING

Poor Mrs. Jones died last winter and left a houseful of kids. After the funeral the pastor spoke to the family:

"How are you all going to manage now that Mother is gone?"

Rachel, the eldest daughter, spoke up:

"We don't really know, Pastor. This is the first time Ma ever died."

# ASHES, ASHES

One evening after supper Charles Barton announced that when he dies he would like to be cremated and have his ashes scattered into the brook that runs through North Harmony. That caused quite a stir in the family.

His son Joe wanted to know how they could go and visit. Charles replied that they could do that quite easily:

Charles: "Just go fishing!"

Joe: "Yes, indeed, but then we couldn't eat the fish we caught!"

His wife objected:

"I won't follow you because I can't even swim, and a life preserver won't do me no good by that point."

A neighbor raised the legal question:

"Environmentally, that may be putting on Higgins Stream more than the stream can handle."

The pastor opined that the Bible makes allowance only for burial:

" 'Ashes to ashes, dust to dust,' says the Good Book."

Huck disagreed:

"The Good Book doesn't allow for burial either, 'cause that would be 'ashes to dust.' "

The whole matter was put to rest by having a second round of coffee.

# REMEMBERING UNCLE EDDIE

According to Huck, Maine adults often smoked.

Huck: "Well, for one thing, it's sociable. Once someone lights up, everybody does, and you all have a lovely afternoon together, I suppose.

"But if you're out in a car, there's nothing you can do. Well, almost nothing. When I was a kid and everybody lit up in the car, I would regularly decide to get sick. And if you didn't put out the cigarettes, I would regularly throw up all over the backseat, and everybody in it. Once, I even hit Uncle Eddie's neck in the driver's seat. Well, of course they'd stop the car and get out. But as soon as I started to feel better, everybody would get back in and light up again. By the time you got there, I would be out of puke, but they still had lots of cigarettes."

Huck was never seen smoking. He explained:

"Around here you just have to breathe and that takes care of the smoking, too."

When he got older he hated even to ride in cars:

"You can smell the cigarette smoke from the people driving by. Heck, I can still smell Uncle Eddy's cigar, and he's been dead for ten years."

# DYIN' HAPPY

Joe Bragdon and Huck fought for years. Although they were really the best of friends, they still liked to kid one another a lot. One day Huck was sitting out on the porch when he spotted Joe coming up the street, about five minutes away. When Joe got up to the porch, Huck asked him:

"Joe Bragdoon! I just been reading the obituaries. You ain't dead yet?"

Joe: "Yes, I am. I died about five minutes ago when I spotted you!"

Huck: "Well, at least you died happy."

The very next day, Huck had one of the kids deliver a nice bouquet of flowers to Joe's house, along with a personal expression of condolences.

When Esther scolded him for the gesture, Huck referred her to a saying from some French saint that he heard from Henri Veilleux:

"The one thing you can't make in this world is an old friend."

## PUTTING SISTER BETH TO REST

Huck's sister Beth finally died from cancer after a long bout. Huck went to the funeral and then took three days off:

"I just had to rest up before going into mourning."

## OLD GEORGE'S EULOGY

Huck was asked to deliver a eulogy at George Flynn's funeral, but to keep it short, perhaps even give one of his memorable one-liners.

Huck: "Old George died as he lived: in his sleep."

# (Just) Livin'

## WHAT'S HAPPENIN'

One summer Huck's sister's boy, Tommy, came up for a visit from Connecticut. After a few hours of sitting around and not doing much, he approached Huck and asked, nervously:

Tommy: So, what's happening?

Huck: Life. Don't you miss it, now!

# MORE THAN JUST LIVIN'?

This fella from the *Hartford Courant* wanted to do a piece about Mainers. It was his misfortune to stumble upon Huck.

Reporter: What do folks do up here in Maine, Mr. Colby?

Huck: Nothin' much.

Reporter: Well, you surely work, don't you?

Huck: Not if we can help it.

Reporter: Let's get more specific: What did you do yesterday?

Huck: I lived.

Reporter: That doesn't sound all that interesting now, does it, Mr. Colby?

Huck: I can't think of anything better, can you?

Reporter: Surely you can. Maybe you went to church, or helped somebody do something, or just went fishing?

Huck: Well, that's all included in what I just said.

Reporter: Now all that 'what you just said' is more than just living, don't you think?

Huck: Hell, no! Ain't nothin' better than just livin'.

# Local Personalities

# THE YORKS

Harry York was a clean man who only drank straight vodka. His wife Francine loved him very much, but preferred gin. She explained:

"Makes your breath smell more innocent."

Harry got his leg shot through in the army. They saved the leg, but it always dripped something brown. He pointed out that the vodka "helped cauterize the wound from the inside."

Francine claimed she didn't really enjoy drinking:

"I got to keep the old man company. And with that leg of his and all . . ."

We never figured out what she meant by that.

Harry and Francine had no children of their own, but adopted one. His name was Fletcher. With all his hair and big nose, he didn't look a bit like his parents.

Harry died and Francine died too. They're buried together in North Harmony. Folks say they were laid out for days without embalming fluid, but I think they're just making fun. Huck claims that at Harry York's funeral, the pastor coined a phrase that all high school graduates learned by heart, at least in that part of Maine:

"Alas, poor York, I knew him well!"

I haven't seen Fletcher in forty years, but he must live somewhere up there on Tower Hill. Unless, of course, he moved down to Connecticut to find a job. Then there's no tellin' where he ended up.

## JOHN POWERS

In the room behind Gramp's barbershop lived a tall strong Indian—a Micmac, I think—named John Powers. He lived there alone, at least some of the time. He had lots of friends, mostly women from neighboring towns and tribes. Evenings they used to practice their war whoops. My grandfather explained:

"That's because they're Indian."

John once said that the rain in North Harmony was special:

"If you look closely after a rain, you'll find money in the grass. It falls with the rain."

And, sure enough, whenever John took me out looking after a rain, I always found a few cents. But when John wasn't there, I just never did find any money.

He said it was his Indian luck.

## SUZIE BRAGDON

Folks never could figure out what Huck did for a living. He, of course, had a garden and did lots of odd jobs, like most everybody else. One day Suzie Bragdon asked Huck to come by and paper her kitchen. Now Suzie was the homeliest thing that ever walked the streets of North Harmony, and that's saying quite a lot. The kids made fun, of course, and the grown-ups often joined in, though I don't know what most of them had to brag about.

Huck: "I didn't need the money; I just wanted to be in Suzie's kitchen," he added with a smile.

Well, he did the kitchen and stayed and finished up the rest of the house as well. When the job was finally over, Suzie agreed with him it was too bad she didn't have more rooms that needed papering.

## LAW ENFORCEMENT: HIKEY'S BIG CASE

Hikey Willis—that's what people called him, though he insisted that his name was Edward A. Willis—anyhow, Hikey was the "constable of North Harmony and Surrounding Precincts." One day he was standing at the four corners writing in a notebook. Huck asked him what he was doing (rumor had it that Hikey couldn't write, and couldn't read either).

Hikey: Don't bother me just now. I'm working on a big case.

Huck: Don't say! So am I.

Hikey: Which one?

Huck: Budweiser.

# I DEPUTIZE YOU

Constable Hikey went into the mill one Friday afternoon to arrest Louis Kennagy. Hikey came out flat on his bottom. He picked himself up and went back in. Again, he came back out on his bottom. He then cornered Jim Hawes as he came out of the grocery store:

Hikey: "I deputize you to go in there and arrest Louis Kennagy."

Well, Jim Hawes did, and he too came out on all fours. Hikey then called in the neighboring state trooper. This time it was Louis that came out on all fours.

Hikey always pointed to this arrest as one his great successes in law enforcement. As he never tired of explaining:

"Things are always easy when you know how to go about it."

# UNCLE WARDELL'S MOVE
# TO SAVE MONEY

None of the old folks drank. Still don't. Father keeps some whiskey in the cupboard, "just in case someone comes by." Only one of the bottles is opened, and it's been twenty years, that I can remember. Father says that nobody drops by anymore because of all those new cars.

Uncle Wardell lost his job and moved to New Hampshire. Liquor's about half price down there because of the taxes. Wardell explains:

"Got to buy it because it's so damn cheap. I saved three dollars and fifty cents just last week!"

To make a long story short, Wardell decided to save himself just about as much money as he could:

"Working in the mill ain't that much fun. And you got to die of something, I suppose."

He did.

# Local News Media

# THE KENNEBEC RIVER

Talk about misprints! A local newspaper reported that, thanks to the Augusta dam's removal, the Kennebec River was now sending up unusual species of fish, such as strippers.

Huck was not impressed, and wrote in to the editor:

"At the Elms Hotel we've had strippers for years."

# WILD TURKEY

Just forty years ago there were no wild turkeys in Maine. Now there are so many that the Department of Game and Fisheries decided to have a lottery and allow a few to be killed. One lucky winner was Dana M. from Harpswell. He shot a turkey and got his picture in the local paper. Although the bird looked as big as Dana, the caption said that he had shot a bird weighing eight and three-quarter pounds.

A friend of Dana's decided to have some fun and had a buddy from Augusta call him up:

"Mr. M., this is Warden Regan from the State Department of Game and Fisheries in Augusta. We see that you have shot a turkey under the legal limit of ten pounds, and you will be subject to the usual penalties."

"But, sir," Dana replied, "that was a misprint. The bird actually weighed eighteen and three-quarter pounds!"

"I am sorry, Mr. M., but we all know that newspapers don't lie."

Dana had no answer to that one.

## DEADLY CAR CRASH

In the local news section, the Portland morning newspaper reported a car crash, in which

"nearly four people were killed."

# NICE LEGS

A couple years after his wife died, Bert Hawkins was feeling lonely. He decided to advertise in the personals section of the North Harmony Weekly:

"Extinguished older man looking for wife. Nice legs."

He received twenty-two inquiries. Three about his extinction, and nineteen about his legs.

# Conversations
# Without Words

# THE MILKMAN

Huck always expected Amos Priest around nine in the morning, when he would pull up in front of the house with all kinds of fresh milk. It took him all that time to milk the cows, fill the glass bottles, and harness up the horse. Fact is, Amos Priest smelled like his horse, but that didn't seem to bother him. Nor did any noise, because he was deaf as a doornail.

Huck: Nice day, Amos!

Amos, hollering out: FIVE CENTS!

Huck always regarded that as an excellent conversation.

## DIGNITY, OR HOW YOU SIT IN YOUR CHAIR

Huck often bragged that his grandparents Emma and Charles Colby had dignity. He told how they used to sit together out on the porch on their straight-back rocking chairs for hours at a time and never speak a word. But when Grandpa would get up and go into the house, Grandma would call something out to him all the way to the kitchen.

Grandpa was hopeful:

"Someday, Emma and I are going to have a fine conversation. But it may not be until after I'm gone out of the room."

Huck noted how good life can be:

"They both died in a car crash. The same one."

Whenever Huck visits their graves, he never fails to comment on how quiet it is in their corner of the cemetery:

"Folks nowadays would be bothered by all the silence. But I always said that the Old Folks sure had dignity."

# Word Plays

# HANGIN' OUT

Once in a while Huck liked to tell jokes, the kind that makes fun of words rather than people. Well, Huck had this friend William from Danbury, Connecticut, who used to come up to Maine to spend summers.

William: Let's go hang out at the new mall this afternoon.

Huck chuckled: I ain't hangin' *that* low.

# TOMORRA

When Huck and Esther's third daughter was born, they thought about naming her Tamara:

"It's such a lovely name; we saw it in a name book!"

Suzie Bragdon visited them at the hospital. As she was leaving, she turned and waved good-bye:

"I'll see ya tomorra."

Huck and Esther looked at one another and right then and there renamed their new daughter Debra.

# Wisdom Words

## JOHN MCCORMACK

Dad had quite a voice when he was young. Right out of high school he went down to Portland and sang for John McCormack himself, who advised him to go to New York City and have a career. So Dad up and went to NYC. He lasted for about six months. When the money ran out he came back to Maine and went to work haying and picking apples.

Huck was amused but said nothing about it all until I was born shortly thereafter. Then he coined another of his memorable phrases that everyone quotes but few understand:

"The tree doesn't fall far from the apple."

Huck maintained that this was the deepest thing he ever said.

## MAKIN' WATER

Hoss Vigue—he was called that, I am told, because he was as big as a horse—was a shy kid who just kept eating and generally avoided girls. His father decided to introduce him to manly exercises and took him into the Elm Street Bar. After a few months of intensive training, Hoss became quite a drinker, but he got even heavier and still avoided the opposite sex.

Huck coined a proverb in his honor:

"You can lead a Hoss to drink, but you can't make him water."

# 'Nuff Said

# A DAY IN HARLEM

Huck made two trips to NYC in his life. The first time, he got off the train too early and ended up in Harlem. Huck later explained his situation:

"I never saw colored people in real life before, except in the minstrel show in North Harmony."

He walked up and down all the streets of Harlem. He later said it felt just like being in a minstrel show, except that now *he* was the one sitting on the end.

When he got back home, he did not attend the minstrel show that year, or ever again. Said he just couldn't figure out why anybody had to sit on the end and get laughed at like that.

# UNCLE GENE'S RETIREMENT

Uncle Gene came home from the army and went to work in the weaving room for Wyandotte Worsted woolen mill. When he retired, he collected his retirement check: a single cash payment of $3,900, which was $100 for each year of service. The mill explained:

"Of course, this is in addition to your Social Security."

He often told stories about the weaving room and the fine plaids they made. About retirement he said little. About Uncle Sam he noted that the security was not very sociable. About the retirement settlement he said nothing.

Nothing at all.

# THE FISHBONE

One day Huck's grandfather Alvey got up from the supper table, put on his hat and coat, and walked out the door, all the way to old Dr. Hanly's house. He seemed to be in a bit of a hurry.

Dr. Hanly: What's the trouble, Alvey?

Alvey: Ahhhhhhhgg!

Dr. Hanly: Oh, you got something caught in your throat? Let's see . . . Yup, I'll get it out. Lie down over here.

Huck lies down and opens his mouth wide:

Dr. Hanly: There, you should be all right now. That'll be twenty-five dollars.

Huck's grandfather slapped a ten down on the table:

Alvey: That's all you're gittin', Doc, and if it's not enough, you can put the damn fishbone right back where you found it.

# Religion

# HAVE A BLESSED DAY!

The religion reporter from the *Connecticut Tribune* came up to interview folks about upcountry religious practices:

Reporter: Mr. Colby, what are your opinions on intermarriage?

Huck: What's that? Aren't *all* marriages *inter*marriages?

Reporter: You know, when someone from one religion gets married with someone from another religion.

Huck: No big deal; most people are Christian up here.

Reporter: And would you say that *you*, Mr. Colby, are Christian?

Huck: Oh, I suppose so.

Reporter: For example, what I mean is, were you born again?

Huck: Once is enough for me!

Reporter: Well, what were your parents?

Huck: Awfully good people.

Reporter: No. I mean religiously.

Huck: Well, Ma was born Catholic and Pa was born Baptist.

Reporter: And which one did you choose?

Huck: I loved *both* my parents!

Reporter: No, I mean which *religion*?

Huck: Well, some Sundays we went to the Baptists, but they looked at us kind of funny. Then we went to the Catholics, and they looked at us kind of funny, too. So we decided that they were more alike than they thought. Most of the Sundays after that we just stayed home and sang hymns with Aunt Jessie. Now you should know that Aunt Jessie was born Catholic and married— excuse me, *inter*married—Uncle Jack, who remained some kind of Protestant. They had a wonderful marriage. They thought that each person was wonderful and that every day was okay, too.

*　　　*　　　*

One day Huck called Uncle Jack, and instead of saying good-bye, Jack said:

"Have a blessed day."

Huck got kind of excited and said:

"Jack, I just told you that my toilet has run all over the floor and I'm out of work and Esther may have to have surgery next week. And you tell me to have a *blessed* day?"

But Jack just repeated his "Have a blessed day" and hung right up as soon as he could.

# VEIL OF TEARS

George Joseph spent a few weeks in Beirut, Lebanon, visiting some old relatives. He told lots of stories when he returned and brought some pictures, too. Huck was concerned:

Huck: Are there many ugly women in Beirut?

George: Not at all. Why do you ask?

Huck: Because some of them have their faces all covered over with veils.

George: No, no, quite the contrary. That's because they are considered beautiful. The veils prevent men from 'casting wanton looks,' as the pastor used to say.

Huck, smiling: That sounds to me like a veil of tears.

Then he added: That's kind of cruel in a warm country like that. Wouldn't it just be nicer for the men to wear hoss-blinders?

# JESUS H. CHRIST!

One day at the shop someone exclaimed "Jesus H. Christ!" about something or other. Huck was in a pensive mood that day:

"I didn't know that Jesus had a middle name. I wonder what it was."

Harold Beecher offered the following:

"I think it was Harold. As in the verse: 'Hark! The Harold-angel sings.'"

Henry Veilleux proposed a French solution:

"His middle name was Jesus *Henry* Christ."

When doubt was expressed, he went on to explain:

"Perhaps you folks have wondered about those letters printed above the cross: INRI. Well, pronounced in French you have *Henri*, which in English is Henry."

Veilleux then went on to deliver his clinching argument:

"If Jesus spoke Hebrew, then he sure as hell spoke French."

# A FRIEND IN JESUS

Our town was a real mixing pot, and Huck was mighty proud of that:

"There were Catlics and 'Piscopalians and Lebanese Arabs and even a few Jews. North Harmony was just that—a place where everyone got along, at least as well as we could. For example, my auntie Jessie loved to sing hymns. This one was her favorite:

"What a friend we have in Jesus!"

When she sang it at the Independence Day celebration, Frank Levine was amused, but joined in, after his own manner:

"What! A *friend* we have in Jesus?"

# Beyond the Pail

Dad and I asked Huck for some off-color stuff, from beyond the pale, so to speak. He imagined (but did he really?) that we had asked for stuff from a *pail*, i.e., a slop pail or chamber mug. So, here goes.

# THE OUTHOUSE AND ITS USES

Charlie Barrett recently purchased a house in town built in 1865 that still had a two-seater outhouse in the backyard. He sought advice from folks at the local Grange about what to do with it. Here is a summary of their ideas:

1) Do nothin'; leave it alone. Who knows when there will be another power outage?

2) Encourage your grandson to use it as a lemonade stand.

3) Tear it down and plant your next crop of tomatoes in the same spot.

4) Transform the two-seater into a single "honeypot" now that your wife has died.

# ESCAPE FROM SHIPWRECK

Uncle Ed bought an old Plymouth right after the war and started a taxi service. To get downtown to the five-and-ten store and back cost fifty cents, thirty cents one way. Huck would mind the phone when there was no one else to do it. Occasionally it fell to his lot to man the taxi as well.

Well, Shipwreck Kelley—no one to this day remembers her real first name—was a fairly hefty woman, weighing in at around three hundred. She had a good disposition and was kindhearted, but she hadn't bothered to wash any part of her body for a number of years. This was obvious to everyone, especially in close quarters like in a taxi. When she would call from downtown for a cab home, Huck could never seem to remember who it was that called. Or he just didn't seem to recognize the person's voice:

Huck: "Someone's waiting for a ride home in front of Sears and Roebuck" was his entire message.

Uncle Ed would do all he could—kept the windows wide open, even smoked a cigar. But nothing seemed to help much.

One day Ed took sick and Huck had to drive the cab. Ed still managed to man the phone:

Ed: "Huck, there's a fare in front of Monkey Wards."

Huck jumped into the car and returned late the next day. Nobody knows where he went or how Shipwreck got home. He claimed that nobody was waiting at Monkey Wards, and since the fish might be biting that day, he decided to "go fishin'," as he always put it. As for Shipwreck, it was rumored that even Amos Priest's horse refused her a ride.

## SMELLIN' THE MUSIC

Huck got a kick out of how Joe Daugier talked about his service in France during the (Second World) War:

Joe: "Their French is very different from mine, and there is a pile of manure in front of every house."

When the war was over he spent a few days in Switzerland:

"My mother always wanted to see where Heidi was from, and I sent her a card."

One morning at the barbershop, folks asked Joe what Switzerland was like.

"I brought home some Swiss air; would you like to smell some?"

And with that he dropped trou, bent forward, and farted out the first line of "Lorelei."

"No problem," he bragged. "I learned that trick in France. It's a specialty over there."

# VIE'S PUNKIN' PIE

Cy Richards didn't talk much, even by Maine standards. Every fall Cy would drive all the way over to Skowhegan to get his squash and pumpkins. After picking, he always stopped off at the Main Street diner to grab a bite to eat. On one occasion an old-timer sitting at the counter told him the following story:

Last fall this fella from Connecticut rushed into the diner and asked to use the bathroom. He said it was urgent:

"Sorry," said Mrs. Tookey, "it's broke and the plumber ain't come by to fix it yet."

Well, this fella rushed out the back door, ran to the punkin' field right behind the diner, cut the top off one of those lovely punkins, and let it all out right inside.

Cy Richards got up from the counter and asked if he could make a quick phone call to his wife:

"Hi, Vie, this is Cy. That *was* shit in the punkin' pie. Bye."

# Huck's Favorite Stories

━━━━━━━━━

These two were among Huck's favorites. I don't think he invented them, though, because I seem to recall somewhat similar ones on the radio a long time ago. I'm going to tell them just the same, in memory of Huck, but I would like to hear from you if you know where they come from. Did Huck invent them himself? He would never say one way or the other, so here goes.

# SPLIT DOG

Joe Daugier had a slender spaniel that was just about the fastest runner in Central Maine, and probably in the entire United States of America. That's what Joe thought, anyhow, and he was going to prove it in live competition. So every morning he took the dog out to train by running him around the barn until the dog just about collapsed.

Well, one day his brother Harry forgot to put away the scythe after haying and left it kind of leaning up against the corner of the barn, with the razor-sharp blade just sticking out into the blue. Joe walked the dog down to the edge of the field and then gave his usual command:

"Go git 'em, boy!"

The dog took off rip-roaring around the barn until he came to the scythe. Joe heard an awful shriek and then a faint yip-yip-yip. When Joe arrived on the scene the dog was split clean up the middle, from head to tail. He leaned over and put his ear to the mouth. "Yip-yip," said the dog faintly. Joe rushed into the barn and came out with an old red flannel shirt and some liquids (some say it was straight turpentine, but who knows?). He doused the dog, bound him up in the shirt, and carefully laid him in his own bed. That night he got up and checked. Yup, there was still a slight yip-yip, so he doused him again real good and pulled the red flannel shirt even tighter.

Well, this went on for what seemed like weeks. When the dog appeared well enough, Joe Daugier announced that the bandages were coming off, and everyone came out to see. But when the shirt was removed, everyone drew back in horror. You see, when Joe in his haste bound up the dog, he put the pieces together wrong, so that now two legs—one front and one rear—were pointed up, and the other two were pointed down!

Well, you can't imagine how disappointed Joe Daugier was, but for old time's sake he decided to take his dog out to the barn again, just to see. They walked on down together, and the dog seemed to be doing just fine on only two legs, perhaps leaning a bit to one side. When they reached the barn and Joe checked to make sure there were no stray scythes around, he yelled out the old command:

"Go git 'em, boy!"

Well, the dog took off like a bat out of hell, of course much slower than before. But when the dog finished the fourth lap, the usual time to stop, a wonderful thing happened: The dog simply flipped over onto his other two legs and took off again with his original speed. He kept it up all morning, always flipping over to his fresh pair of legs when he got tired.

"Well," said Joe, "he'll be no damn good in the hundred meters, but somewhere there must be a long-distance marathon for dogs."

## SPORTIN' AT THE GRANGE ONE SATURDAY EVENING

Ben Farnsworth heard that there were lots of women at the Saturday-evening Grange dances and decided to give it a try. He looked around the room and noticed a plain-looking woman sitting in the corner with a kind of glint in her eye.

Ben: Ben Farnsworth.

Woman: Sally Fraker.

Ben: Would you like to dance?

Sally: Don't mind if I do.

As they began to dance, the music got faster and faster until, on one of the turns, Sally's artificial eye popped right out. Without losing a step, Ben reached out and caught it on the fly.

Sally: Much obliged!

Ben: Oh, don't mention it.

The evening was lovely and Ben ended up sportin' the night away at Sally's place. The next morning at breakfast, Ben said what fun it had all been.

Ben: But tell me, Sally, do you spend the night with everyone you meet at the dance?

Sally: No, siree. Only with those who catch my eye.

# Not Yet

The spirit of these upcountry tales taps into a well-known anecdote about a Connecticut newspaper fella who wanted to discover and report on what is so special about livin' in Maine. He found himself a local sage and nervously led off his interview as follows:

"Sir, have you lived here all your life?"

The answer, now proverbial, startled him:

"Not yet."

Indeed, an alternative title of this Huck collection might well have been: *Not Yet*, or even *Not Dead Yet*. Here are a few more samples.

# TOMATOES?

Huck was out tending his garden. A tourist pulled over and tried to start up a conversation.

Tourist: Are we are going to have lots of tomatoes this year?

Huck: Most likely.

Tourist: When?

Huck: When they are ripe.

# BLUEBERRYING

Granddaughter: Where is Grandma?

Grandfather: She went out to pick blueberries.

Granddaughter: But it's not blueberry season yet.

Grandfather: She'll be gone for a while, then.

# BEST TOY

I asked Huck what toys he remembered from his childhood.

Huck: I especially remember a peg-board set.

T. Amony Perky: What did you learn from it, Huck?

Huck: Just about everything!

T. Amony Perky: How old were you when you got it?

Huck: Oh, I never actually *got* one. Not yet, anyhow.

T. Amony Perky: . . .

Huck: But I still remember *wanting* one something awful.

## SICK AND SAD?

Huck once got the flu and was lying in bed, sad as hell. His mother wondered why:

"It's bad enough being sick, Huck. Do you have to be sad too?"

From that moment on Huck Colby was hardly ever sad again. And when his cancer was coming on and he was having a rough day, he quietly liked to notice:

"I may be sick but I am not dead yet."

# BABY HAROLD

Huck had three grandchildren from his daughter Paula: Sam, the oldest, Isaac, and Baby Harold. Harold died of crib death when he was only six months old.

When Isaac started school, the teacher asked the students if they had any brothers and sisters.

Isaac: "I have two brothers: Harold, who died, and Sam, who isn't dead yet."

At Christmastime, the family sings that old hymn with special devotion and intention:

"Hark! The Harold-angel sings."

CPSIA information can be obtained
at www.ICGtesting.com
Printed in the USA
BVHW060848210819
556377BV00001B/2/P

9 780578 507637